Impactful Leadership

Wes Lee

Published by Wes Lee, 2020.

While every precaution has been taken in the preparation of this book, the publisher assumes no responsibility for errors or omissions, or for damages resulting from the use of the infor-mation contained herein.

IMPACTFUL LEADERSHIP

First edition. August 20, 2020.

Copyright © 2020 Wes Lee.

Written by Wes Lee.

I dedicate this book to you, I have so much appreciation for you, and your dedication to yourself inspires me.

Contents

Table of Contents

INTRODUCTION 7

DISCOVERING YOUR LEADERSHIP STYLE 9

STEP 1: STEPPING INTO THEIR WORLD WITH APPRECIATION 34

STEP 2: DISCOVERING WHAT MOVES A PERSON 54

STEP 3: BREAK THE CYCLE 70

STEP 4: MAKE A PROBLEM SOLVABLE 76

STEP 5: CREATE ALTERNATIVES THAT EMPOWER 93

STEP 6: CONDITIONING NEW BEHAVIOR 112

STEP 7: CULTIVATE A NEW ENVIRONMENT & TIE IT TO THEIR GREATEST PURPOSE 119

A LEVEL OF PERSONAL HONESTY 138

BONUS: *YOU ARE RICH* 139

Introduction

Impactful Leadership is a 7-step execution plan designed to take you by the hand from discovering your leadership style, to expanding your depth and reach as a leader. The core of this system focuses on human needs; how to lead people to a higher quality of life by helping them meet their deepest necessities. Impactful Leadership is practical and action-oriented. You'll engage in thought exercises, reflection, and take actions to help you discover yourself and the needs of others. In this way, each copy of the book is different for every person, because each person who goes through the book will have a different experience.

Impactful Leadership contains ample opportunities to journal and contribute to the pages, making it a living document that grows as you grow. By the end of the book, you'll have a leadership framework to apply to the nearly endless array of personal challenges we face. I encourage you to try Impactful Leadership, follow the seven steps, and discover yourself within its pages.

With Deep Gratitude,

Wes

Step 1: Discovering Your Leadership Style

What is Leadership?

The best place to begin our journey is with an understanding of effective Leadership and why we make the decisions we make. The most effective leaders create permanent change and transform lives with their actions.

Leadership is a learned skill, and everybody can be an impactful leader. Everyone is a leader, from parents who want to impact their children to volunteers who hunger to contribute to their community. Any person who wants to be a beacon of light for people can lead, and every day is overflowing with opportunities to rise to your potential!

As we begin this exciting journey together, we'll dive into a new way of viewing Leadership that I've learned and put into practice for years. This book celebrates the phenomenal work performed in human needs psychology trademarked by Tony Robbins. For our purpose, Leadership will focus on our ability to influence other people by discovering what already influences their behaviors, emotions, actions, thoughts, and feelings.

I want you to visualize yourself, making a tremendous impact on people. You can imagine a single person, a group of people, your team members at work, or anyone in your life whom you want to influence. What if you had the skills to take these people you visualize and move them to achieve outstanding results in their lives and change for the greater good? How fulfilled would you feel to shift these people and know that you lead them to exceptional results?

For the past ten years, I've been on a mission to grow and introduce success into every fiber of people's lives. In my quest, I wrote a best-selling course that's reached 40 countries and counting. And, I've worked with some of the most elite fortune 500 companies, in industries from real estate to technology. What I can say confidently is that we all have habits that are at the core of who we are.

When you learn to apply these timeless principles into your own life, you'll equip yourself to transform your quality of life. You'll lead other people to shift their thinking, the way they feel, actions they take, and ultimately their life. And Your ability to move people is your mark as a leader. Let's Begin!

HUMAN NEEDS PSYCHOLOGY™

Developed by Tony Robbins and refined by Cloé Madanes: Human Needs Psychology™ is a discipline focused on the absolute needs that each of us shares as human beings. It doesn't matter if a person is a radical, royalty, homeless, middle class, black, white, red, orange, sick or healthy, young or old. We'll utilize this psychology as the base to propel your ability to lead and make massive progress with yourself and others. Sound great? The goal of this discipline is to uncover new choices, behaviors, actions, thoughts, and feelings that a person may not have known they have within them. We'll impact people in ways that feel good to them, and help them meet their deepest needs, by introducing new and enlightening ways to get what they desire.

How do we Make Decisions?

Life doesn't "happen" to us. We create our lives, and it's our decisions that shape our lives. So, how do we make decisions that create our lives? We're making three decisions every second of every day, which affect us in the interim and over the long term.

How are you using your body? Such as your breathing, how tall you sit or stand, and how you move.

Where's your focus? What you're focused on is what you

feel at any moment.

Did you notice that 1 & 2 are non-verbal? The third factor is: what words do we assign to an experience? The language we assign to an experience determines how we feel. If you say: "That makes me **mad**!" you're right, and you'll feel it. If you say: "That makes me **happy,**" you're also right, and you'll also feel it.

When we're in distress or pain, it's because we're inwardly focused. And one or all of the above three factors are off. The fantastic part is that you're in control of all three! And the more robust these three factors are, the more significant you'll feel. You'll also make more empowering or less empowering decisions.

Example

If someone's having difficulty, you can focus on the problem or be the solution. Ask yourself, "how can I contribute to this person right now?"

Pay attention to the language you use, and that other people use. We can use enhanced or diminutive language. Let's say someone asks you, "How's your day?" you can choose to respond: "Good," or you can enhance your language and say, "Phenomenal." Do you think you'll feel different depending on how you respond? Or let's say you or another person encounters a tough situation. Does it "Suck" or is it "Inconvenient." This is diminutive language; we're adopting a style that's less harsh and negative.

Lastly, the quickest way to instantly affect your mood at any given moment is to change how you use your body by changing your physiology. If you or another person is sitting, stand up. If you feel down, take deep breaths. Go for a walk, stretch out, or pay attention to the foods and drinks you put into your body that day. These all positively affect your body and your state, which enables you to be more effective in making significant decisions.

How we Shape Our World

It's no secret that each of us is unique and superior in certain aspects of life. We're also inferior in other dimensions, making us all even. Now, you already understand the three decisions we're making every second, that affect us in the interim (short term). Next are the factors that affect our life over a long period. How we perceive the world, what it means to us, and how it affects our decisions.

Each of us is After Six Human Necessities:

1. We want to feel certain

2. We want variety and a sense of change

3. We all want to feel like we matter

4. We want to experience love and feel connected

5. We each want to feel as though we're growing

6. We want to contribute to something beyond ourselves

Each of us Has a Map to Guide us to our Desired Necessities

1. We have universal beliefs about the way life is

2. We each have desires and fears

3. We each have methods we rely on to meet our necessities

4. We all have boundaries for ourselves (Thresholds)

5. We have situations in which we would violate our

thresholds

6. We have a belief system about who we are

7. We all have preferences in how we make decisions
   Ex: (Big Picture vs. Detail-oriented)

Each of us Has Emotions we Default to

These emotions can be emotions that give us strength or make us weaker. Reflect on yourself for a moment; what are your go-to feelings? When I was growing up, I lived in an emotional frame of anger. If I didn't like something, I'd get angry. Even If something happened that I wanted, sometimes I'd get mad because I wouldn't feel worthy of that kind gesture. So, where do you go to often within yourself?

Six Human Necessities

What's fascinating is that we meet these necessities in ways that help us and harm us. Every person has a way to meet these necessities, however. As leaders, we want to discover how a person is getting their needs met. We need to influence them to achieve their needs in ways that are pleasurable and positive over the long term of their life. Make sense? So why do you think a person would do something harmful such as drink or do drugs? Why do addictions even happen? I used to believe it was the drug itself (which plays a factor!). However, an enlightening moment occurred for me when I realized that it has more to do with *us* than the outside stimulus. People in my family had drug problems, and wisdom taught me that the drugs were meeting several of their necessities. If that drug meets enough needs, it creates an addiction. What are the three essential needs a drug addict wants? Write three of the six.

1.

2.

3.

We're each unique in the way we value these necessities. Every person is different and meets these in different ways. You'll know your essential needs in a stressful experience. We tend to value a couple of these needs over the others; however, we still require all six. So, which two showed up for you the last time you experienced a challenging situation? For me: I value growing, and I appreciate the feeling of significance. I get anxious when I feel like I'm not growing, and I highly value feeling like I matter. The combination of those necessities is why you're reading this material.

Our Guiding Map

Are you meeting your needs? How do you know if you are? What do you believe?

What thresholds have you placed on yourself to achieve your essential necessities?

Your Default Emotions

Do you remember the last time you expressed an emotion quicker than you could think? We act on our feelings, which positively or negatively affect our quality of life.

Recap
Ask yourself these three questions throughout the day:

1. What meaning do I choose to give this situation?
2. What action am I going to take?
3. What do I choose to focus on right now?

Understanding Yourself First

Before leading other people, it's critical to know how you perceive the world and how your perspective interacts with another person's view of the world. Expanding your understanding of yourself brings you the ability to develop your influence and knowledge of other people, giving your life more options and flexibility.

If you want to impact anyone and shift their

perspective to make positive changes, you have to understand what already motivates them. We can't effectively change a person for our reasons. Leadership means understanding how they see the world and how you can help them meet their necessities for their purposes.

Have you ever had someone tell you all of the reasons why you should change? Did you resist changing? Unless you were after the same necessities as that person, you probably resisted it because they didn't understand how you see the world.

How Happiness Works

Do you know why you get upset or frustrated, and why you feel ecstatic in certain parts of your life? When I learned and applied this, it was mind-blowing and straightforward! There are two factors we can shift to achieve happiness and take ourselves out of a painful state of being:

1. We have the control to change our situation

2. We have the power to change the narratives in our mind

Example

My wife and I, at the time of this writing, live in Hawaii. I highlight this because this is the most fulfilling area of my life. It's the most fulfilling area because our marriage exceeds my perception of marriage. I always imagined marrying my best friend, what I never envisioned was living in such a beautiful place and making life into a wondrous adventure! So, because my marriage exceeds what I imagined, I'm thrilled!

Now, let's look at the other side of this. When I was a teenager, I didn't have money, and I didn't have a relationship or a place of my own to live. My situations (Relationship, Finances, and Living) didn't match how I perceived things should be. In my mind, I wanted lots of money, a great relationship, and a beautiful place to call mine. Because I had none of those, what could I have done? I could have changed my situation and started aggressively going after what I wanted. Or I could have changed the way I perceived being single, with no income or a place of my own. I could have said, "I'm working on myself, so I can have everything I desire." Instead of "I'm not worthy of having the things I desire," Can you see the power in this small shift? Change the situation or change the way you perceive the situation.

Action Steps

1. Where are you thrilled in your life right now? What pleases you about it the most? Pay attention and write down IF your expectations meet or exceed the situation.

2. What area of your life do you want to improve in the most? What doesn't please you about it? Do your expectations meet how you imagine it should be? How can you use this information to change it?

3. What are your top two human necessities of the six? Take ownership of them. Think of them as your best friends, and feel proud because they are your primary drivers (Think about which necessities you live and embody each day).

7 Steps to Impactful Leadership

If we want to lead another person or group of people, we need to ask ourselves:

1. What are their necessities, and what are their desires?

2. How can you help them get to their destination?

3. What roadblock(s) are preventing them from getting where they want?

    - What is their guiding map? What beliefs do they hold, and what emotions do they default to habitually?

    - How do they represent themselves to me? (How they show up)

Remember, we all desire the same six human necessities. What varies is the paths we take to get them. The actions we take are for our reasons, no one else's. Everything you're learning takes work and practice. But it's worth it! Because you'll expand your ability to influence, and you'll transform yourself into a more effective leader of change and progress.

7 Steps to Impactful Leadership

First Step: Stepping into their world with appreciation

Second Step: Discovering what moves a person

Third Step: Break a person's cycle

Fourth Step: Make a problem solvable

Fifth Step: Create alternatives that empower

Sixth Step: Conditioning new behavior

Seventh Step: Cultivate a new environment & Tie it to their highest purpose

Step 1: Stepping Into Their World With Appreciation

If you want to lead someone to change, you have to understand their desires. It's their desires that will move them to change, not yours.

- Where is the person at, and what is the context behind their situation?

- Which of the six human necessities are most important to them?

- What is their guiding map?

- What do they believe they need to do to meet their core human necessities?

- Who is this person? What shapes them?

- Listen to them with curiosity. What can you appreciate about the person?

- Take action and anticipate. You can't help anyone by being passive.

- Take your time and build rapport.

- What is the person's response when you challenge them and push back?

- What do they believe? What thresholds (rules) have they imposed on themselves?

Step 2: Discovering What Moves a Person

Influencing ourselves and other people begins by searching for the motivation that's already present within each of us. What challenges do you want to overcome? What is the desired result? It's the desire that will push you and others to overcome any problem.

- First, you must build rapport. This foundation will allow you to challenge and push another person, by showing them that changing their situation is a **must**.

- Use reciprocity. "If I do **X** for you, Will you do **X** for me?"

- Discover the hidden force that moves this person to meet their deepest needs. It could be anything. A great place to start is with: *Love*

- Show them that continuing in the direction they're going means pain or continued pain, and shifting from their pattern will mean happiness.

- What moves each person will vary, it could be anything from family, to death, to their self-image.

Step 3: Break a Person's Cycle

We all have habitual patterns that we follow, like music playing on repeat. When we interrupt the "music" playing in our head, we open ourselves up for something new.

- Once again, it's a must to have a person's respect and rapport. Our goal is to serve others humanely.

- How can you change the context, or parts of the context, of a situation?

- What is causing them pain? What do they have that you can utilize to make changing their situation necessary?

- Regularly change direction in the conversation. Become unpredictable and mercurial. Change the pace, the tone, and the focus, changing trends frequently breaks a person's cycle.

- Ask questions to discover what already motivates a person.

- Introduce new ways of feeling, thinking, and behaving that are contrary to how the person currently is.

Step 4: Make a Problem Solvable

When people are facing a challenge, they often view it as something overwhelming. Do you know that feeling of overwhelm? You may have said to yourself, "This is impossible" or "There's no way I can do this." Either it was the language you were using, or you weren't specific enough in identifying the situation.

- What emotion does the person lack that you

can bring back?

- When someone tells you about their challenge, ask them for an example. Listen for your opportunity to define what's holding them back at their root.

- What they think is holding them back, is usually not the root cause.

- How can you solve their issue? Define a new outcome for them.

- Listen to the needs they express and what they believe. You'll know how to proceed, based on what they believe is essential.

- How can you shape their challenge into something solvable?

Step 5: Create Alternatives That Empower

Remember this fundamental principle: Everyone is trying to meet specific necessities. We can't remove the vehicle that fits their beliefs and needs, without filling that space with a more empowering alternative that meets or exceeds what they need. If we influence a person to change their negative behavior, and we don't replace it, another negative response will. You wouldn't want an alcoholic to stop drinking and form an eating addiction, would you? I've witnessed it happen many times. Reflect on this:

- Embrace new beliefs, habits, thoughts, and actions. One of my empowering activities is that I start my day at 4 a.m.

- What are past moments where you felt utterly unstoppable? You can also ask this to a person you want to help. This question will summon those feelings again.

- Who do you look up to as a model? Surround yourself with people who have what you want. Whether those people mentor you online or in-person, this becomes your empowering environment.

Step 6: Conditioning New Behavior

Repetition is how we reinforce ourselves. Consistent reinforcement will create conditioning.

- You create your compelling future. Reinforce it with constant reminders—place reminders around your home about your future.

- Create an environment that supports and reinforces your new habits. For example, my wife and I wanted to learn to speak publicly, so we surrounded ourselves with a group of Toastmasters.

- Your new pattern becomes routine with consistency and allowing yourself to pour your emotions into it.

- Your new thought, emotion, or action must have a future. Similar to conditioning children for the future, you're conditioning this new pattern for its future in your life. Start small and gradually build the habit over time.

Remember: How do you eat an elephant? One bite at a time.

Step 7: Cultivate a New Environment & Tie it to Their Highest Purpose

Humans need love; our desire for love is our most powerful motivator to change.

- Is the person receiving pain or pleasure in their current environment?

- Reinforcing a person's highest purpose will give them the strength to overcome the harshest environments.

- Does their environment support their new behavior?

- Create a new environment for the person

- Is there life reinforcing their new environment in a pleasurable or painful way?

- How can a change meet the needs of more than one person? <u>You have to trust that you already know these things.</u>

- These happen naturally when our mind, heart,

and body invest in serving others.

Step 1: Stepping into Their World With Appreciation

If we want to motivate anyone, we have to drive them for their reasons, not ours.

- Which of the six necessities do they value the most?

- How do they meet their needs?

- What habitual patterns of emotion is their default?

How a Person Determines if They're Meeting Their

Necessities

We all have particular distinctions in how we create meaning in our lives. What makes us one of a kind is how we try to achieve these necessities. Only you can decide if you're meeting your core necessities.

Universal Beliefs – Beliefs we hold about "how" life is.

Example:

What's your meaning of life? Death? Money? Love?

Whom you believe you are – This is your collection of life experiences that have shaped your belief system about how you see yourself.

Example:

What script do you run every day in your head, and what qualities do you see in others that don't align with you? Whom do you admire? How are you similar to your role model(s)? How are you unique from your role model(s)? What do you believe your life's meaning is?

Your Boundaries – We consider our boundaries when we're deciding how to get the feeling we want. We each have different personal limits.

Example:

What should I have? What shouldn't I have? Something is impossible vs. anything is possible. What will you do? What will you never do? What do you believe is necessary for your life, and what you will never accept? These are self-imposed rules you place on yourself.

How you meet your needs/What method you use – This is how we meet our needs. We all use underlying vehicles to get what we desire. These come in different flavors, and they can be positive, negative, or neither positive nor negative.

Example:

Reflect on how you meet your needs. What do you use? If you want to feel like you matter, how do you achieve that necessity? Maybe you use money, or the gym, or your work. Do you meet your needs with positive, negative, or neutral methods?

Contextual Beliefs – Every day, we're faced with a lot of different situations, which require our evaluation. These are beliefs we hold about how to evaluate the context.

Example:

You may believe it's wrong to steal; at the same time, you may think that taking food to feed your family is ok. These beliefs are contexts when you would break your boundaries.

What you move towards or away from – We're motivated to avoid feelings of pain or gain feelings of pleasure. These two forces are behind our decisions in a context.

Example:

Are you moving Towards Feelings of pleasure: What draws you towards the situation?

Avoiding feelings of pain: What's something you'll never accept for your life?

Filters people use to process the world – Can two of the same experiences, be different? In reality, it's the same experience. It's each of our personal and unique filters that make the same experience different. You can utilize these filters, to help a person make more effective decisions, by providing information in a way that a person processes it.

Example:

We have several different filters for viewing the world. One is the trees vs. the forest. When we lead people, some of these people will prefer the information delivered with as much detail as possible. These are the people we call "The Trees." On the other hand, some people prefer the overview and don't care as much about the small details. These are the people we call "The Forest." If you wanted to influence the *trees* effectively, you wouldn't give them a summary, would you? And if you tried to affect the forest, you wouldn't get into the specific details, right?

Leadership Principles Organized

First Organizing Principle: How we Shape Our World

Each of us is After Six Human Necessities:

1. We want to feel certain
2. We want variety and a sense of change
3. We all want to feel like we matter
4. We want to experience love and feel connected
5. We each want to feel as though we're growing
6. We want to think that we are contributing to something beyond ourselves

Each of us Has a Map to Guide Our Six Human Necessities

1. We have universal beliefs about the way life is
2. We each have desires and fears
3. We each have methods we rely on to meet our

necessities

4. We all have boundaries for ourselves (Thresholds)

5. We have situations in which we would violate our thresholds

6. We have a belief system about who we are

7. We all have preferences in how we make decisions Ex: (Big Picture vs. Detail-oriented)

Each of us Has Emotions we Default to

These emotions can be emotions that give us strength or make us weaker. Reflect on yourself for a moment. What's a feeling that you go to often? When I was growing up, I lived in an emotional frame of anger. If something happened and I didn't like it, I'd get angry. If something happened that I wanted, I'd also get mad because I wouldn't feel worthy of that kind gesture. So, what feeling(s) do you go to often within yourself?

Second Organizing Principle
How We Make Decisions

1. How do you use your body?
2. Where do you focus your attention?
3. What positive/negative words do you assign to an experience?

Third Organizing Principle

What Influences Us

1. How do our close relationships influence us?

2. How does our world around us, our work, and our goals affect us?

3. How do we change ourselves?

What is Your Most Potent Force?

What influences us more than any other internal or external force, is living consistently with whom we believe we are. Each of us has a deep need to stay congruent with how we define ourselves. Grasping this concept will help you identify what influences and motivates the people in your life. To understand what guides their decisions, listen to what they say (Their words), and how they say it (Their tonality).

People act congruently with whom they believe they are.

Also, what can you appreciate about the

person? Foster mutual respect comes from your genuine appreciation of other people. Sincere appreciation isn't something you can fake; it has to come from your soul. So, next time you're with someone, ask yourself: "What can I appreciate about them right now?" When you do this, you step outside of yourself, and you make yourself unable to judge and criticize someone. Remember: You can't effectively lead or influence if you're judgmental.

The Part our Emotions Play

Each person has a couple of emotions that they regularly lean on. Each person also has a predictable way of using their words, and they have patterns within their environment. To discover what these are, ask yourself:

- How do they use their language? How do they use their body, where's their focus?

- How does their environment help them meet their necessities?

- What emotions do they regularly come back to, and which emotions dominate?

A lot of your influence will happen behind the scenes.

Activity

Roleplay this activity with a close family member or friend using the six necessities.

Our Deepest Necessities

1. Which two necessities do you value the most, and which two are the least important?

2. Which necessity do you value the most in a context? (Unique Situations that come up in your life)

Our Map

Desires and Fears

- What do you need to feel fulfilled?

- What do you avoid to protect yourself from pain?

- What is it you want from your life?

Universal Beliefs

- What gives you the greatest feelings of love in your life?

- What is the primary purpose of a relationship?

- What is the most significant source of pleasure in life? What is the most significant cause of pain?

Who We Are

- Who do you believe you are?

- How do you represent yourself in public? Is it different than at home?

- Whom do you admire, and why? Who do you never want to be like, and why?

Our Self-Imposed Boundaries

- What rules do you set for your life?

- What are your musts for your life?

- What must others never do?

Thresholds

- When would you break the rules you've set for yourself?

- Describe a time when you held back expressing yourself.

- Do you filter your behaviors?

How we Filter Our Decisions

- How often do you make decisions based on fear? If you had to be honest with yourself.

- What emotions drive your decisions the most? Positive, Negative, and Neutral?

- What are your daily habits? Where do you devote most of your time?

How we Meet Our Necessities

- What do you use to meet your core necessities?

- What gives you feelings of assuredness?

- Variety?

- Connection?

- A sense of growth?

- Service and contribution?

Step 2: Discovering What Moves A Person

When a person reaches their threshold, and change becomes a **MUST**-instead of something that would be nice to have- They'll make the necessary shift. People move for their reasons, and one of your goals as a leader is to discover what drives them to the point of action!

These are the best paths to accomplish this:

1. It must be a rapid change. The person must make the connection:

    - Not changing = Continued pain

    - Changing = Relief and pleasure

2. Discover what moves a person by discovering what necessities they're trying to obtain, and what their map roadmap is to get them.

3. Once you step into their world with a sense of

appreciation, you'll be able to tailor your approach to lead and serve them.

4. Be patient, and stay with them. It may take a couple of tries and some searching.

5. What moves people depends on the individual. One approach won't work on everyone. Some people may be driven by family, while animals may move others. Utilize questions to drive to the heart of the person.

This practice takes a heart for service. You'll be looking beyond yourself to the deepest parts of their soul. Once you understand them better than they know themselves, you'll be in a position to guide them towards more empowering actions for their life. In this step, the skills you'll gain are:

- Connecting with a person's belief system

- Effectively framing situations

The Path to Influence

We want to lead a person to create rapid results that last. To impact people in a lasting way:

1. We can change their actions in a situation.
2. We can change their feelings.

How do we change their actions or emotions? With the three decisions, we're always making.

1. We can help them change how they're using their body.
2. (Breathing, Posture, Diet)
3. We can help them improve the words they're using, which define their experiences.
4. We can help them change the focus of their attention.

Connecting With A Belief System

When a person has a behavior they need to change, they usually hold firmly to that behavior because it's meeting several of their core necessities. They believe that changing this behavior will cause them more pain, and they'll lose what's meeting their needs. It even goes for low-level needs, where their actions are destructive. To create a lasting shift in any person, you need to discover what already influences them. Because that influence is what they'll place more value on than their pain.

Demonstrate the impact their behavior is causing and find a solution. In creating a new routine that meets the person's necessities at higher levels, you give them pleasure and empower them.

Personal Example

At a very young age, I was around drug-dealers and some terrible people. Theft, eviction, assault, and dysfunction were regular occurrences in my childhood. Faced with these challenges, around eight years old, I made a decision that has shaped the course of my life. I realized: I can either join this or rise above it. The pain of being left home alone for days, hunger, and a lack of resources were forging me under fire. I began working out at a very young age, so I could become strong enough to protect the people I love. I also developed the belief that I will rise above this life I live, and nothing will stop me. I'm grateful for the emotional intensity of that time in my life. I carry that same belief today, and I've learned to focus it into an intense work ethic that surpasses most people. As I write this: I work at least 50 hours a week, take 12 College Credits, operate two businesses, and am writing this for you. I wake up at 4 A.M. seven days a week, and I don't stop until 9 – 11 P.M, I found an empowering meaning, from a disempowering environment.

Effective Framing Techniques

With different feelings, comes a different meaning. You can see the context in many different ways. To change how the context:

1. Setup an interaction, by first directing a person's attention, in the direction we want them to focus, then tell them what this will mean for them.

    - "**X** *is what I want you to focus on, and* **X** *is*

what this will mean to you."

2. Take a person's pre-existing situation, and show it to them in a different way, that they didn't see it.

- "They took your money; they can never take your knowledge and experience."

3. Take a person's situation and destroy it. We kill it by contrasting it.

- "You may be overweight, but there are people in the hospital praying to beat cancer."

How to Frame

1. **Connection:** Before utilizing framing techniques, you must have a relationship with the person. Have you ever had someone, with no rapport, try to tell you why you need to do something? I bet you didn't do it, did you?

2. **Break the Person's Cycle:** Sharing a story or asking a question that they weren't expecting changes the frame of the interaction.

3. **Ask Questions**: The most significant benefit to questions is that they cause people to search themselves for the answers.

4. **Change how the person uses their body**: Have them move from sitting to standing, take deep breaths, get them yelling, clapping, snapping their fingers. Use anything that causes the body to do something different.

Directing a Person's Attention

You're creating the frame, in advance, for how the interaction will go and what you want people to focus on and internalize. This discipline focuses on how you <u>set up</u> what you want people to hear, instead of figuring out <u>what to say</u>.

Example: "By the end of our time together, you'll feel empowered. (This is the setup) If we're going to work together, I need to know, are you committed to changing? Because we're not going to waste each other's time if you're only in this half-way.

(They'll say they commit) Since you're investing in the process, we're going to get you results." (Another Setup)

In this way, you've set the standard that they will feel empowered and get the results, as long as they commit. They'll get the results, but not necessarily because of you. They'll get the results because they will work harder to stay consistent with their commitment to change.

How to Direct Their Attention

1. Ask questions you already know the answer to, so you can guide them.

2. Always direct their attention to how this benefits them.

Scrambling a Person's Situation

We're taking a context and changing its meaning, by scrambling it in the person's head. Two effective ways to accomplish this are by utilizing comparison and contrast.

Two Effective Scrambles:

1. **Scramble the specific situation**: If they see the narrative as a problem, you can show them how it's a solution.

    - **Example**: "I lost a huge client today; this hurt my business!"

    - **Scramble**: "That client was very threatening, can you imagine how fortunate you are, that the client left before any lawsuits occurred?"

2. **Scramble thoughts about the situation:** Change the way they remember the case or introduce new information that changes their perspective of the situation.

- **Example:** "My boss sat me down and yelled at me today for poor performance."

- **Scramble**: "Imagine he sounded like Shrek, wore a huge pair of suspenders, and smoked a big cartoon cigar."

How to Effectively Scramble

1. Be sure to agree with them and their beliefs. Even if you disagree, you could appreciate their intent, couldn't you? Don't judge them. You can't lead if you're judging.

2. Break their perpetual cycle of emotions and behavior

3. Ask questions. Questions are non-threatening and non- invasive. Questioning causes people to search for answers within themselves.

Destroy a Situation by Utilizing Contrast

Contrast destroys a frame of reference, which is especially useful when working with negative behavior. Use this variation to cause a monumental shift in focus.

Example: Let's say you're a teacher, and another teacher is complaining to you about their job. You can destroy their frame of reference by saying, "I spoke with one of our foreign students, who said they're grateful to learn from you because they don't have schools in their country."

Example: Let's say you want your children to eat their vegetables. You can destroy their frame of reference by saying, "I met a person today, who told me they'd love some peas because they haven't eaten in three days."

Action Steps

Find three people who are experiencing challenges in their life right now. (There's no shortage) How can you utilize what you've learned to elevate them into a better state? Use these effective framing techniques with them and capture your observations and realizations here.

1.

2.

3.

Step 3: Break The Cycle

Humans are habitual creatures. To lead anyone to lasting change, all we need to do is break their regular cycles of emotion and behavior. When we break these cycles that people go into, it introduces space within them for a new feeling or action to replace the old one.

Remember: Until we break their old habits, we can't introduce new ones.

Where does the person already express strength? When we discover where people are already doing well, we can lend that strength to other parts of their life that lack power. Once we bring vitality into a weak area of their lives, we'll condition it to stick as a new habit.

As always, before breaking their cycles, we must have a high degree of respect, rapport, and mutual connection.

Which Habitual Patterns Are we Breaking?

1. We're breaking what they habitually focus on

2. We're breaking the words they usually associate with situations

3. We're breaking their cycle for how they're using their body

For example, One of the most excellent tools to break the cycle of focus is to be outrageous. You need to "violate" what most people consider polite. These include:

- Sexual topics

- Confusing topics

- Disgusting topics

- Strange noises and use of your body

- Anything you can think of that's unexpected

The most important distinctions to rapidly change words include:

Awareness

People are mostly unconscious of their behavior, including the words they use. There's tremendous power when you make a person conscious of emotions or actions.

Example: If they say: "This sucks!" You can make them aware by saying: "Does this suck, or is it a little inconvenient?"

Asking Questions

In this context, the best questions are the most obscene and outrageous questions. Challenge what they believe is sensible and logical. You'll gain powerful insights into what's going on, and it's an incredible tool to break their regular cycles.

Getting to The Root

Some of these habits are ruining people's quality of life. When we break a habit, it needs to be replaced by a more empowering practice. If it's not, the problem will find a new vehicle.

Example: One of my closest family members broke a terrible drug addiction. It was a battle for years, and I'm proud of the courage and strength they demonstrated. After cutting the dependence, they never replaced the habit with something that would meet their necessities at a higher level. So, instead of doing hard drugs, they drank alcohol a lot more often. Alcohol became the replacement because they didn't get to the root.

The root of the issue will always have some emotional habit related to:

- How they use their words

- How they use their body

- What they're focused on

Once you break their regular cycle, you bring their behaviors to the conscious mind. You're empowering people to change by giving them awareness. You'll provide them with the control they need to create new habits that are good for them and meet their necessities at much higher levels.

Action Step

I want you to remember a time when you were feeling negative emotions. Close your eyes and connect with those feelings. Put yourself back into that negative place, consciously, and use these tools to bring yourself back out of it. Play with your emotions on this.

Example: I remembered a time, during my service in the Army when I was angry. Some people had different personality types than myself, so we didn't mix well. I remembered the exact moment where I was at the peak of my anger. I could feel the way I felt that day. I scrambled that same situation, by imagining it as a cartoon and imagining everyone looking like Oompa-Loompas. I broke the anger because I visualized an entirely different experience. Try it for yourself!

Step 4: Make a Problem Solvable

You've stepped into their world with a sense of appreciation (Step 1). You used your newly found rapport and respect to discover what moves them and utilize that to help them change (Step 2). You broke their regular cycle of how they're using their body, how they're using their words, and what they're focusing their attention on (Step 3). Now you need to define their problem in a way that it can be solved (Step 4).

What often happens is that people take small problems and make them way too big. They also take significant issues and make them unimportant. Whatever challenges a person is facing, their source of frustration often comes from the way they define the problem; as impossible. Either they haven't pinpointed the real challenge, or they adopted a belief that they can't fix a problem.

Help a person solve their problem and get results by taking them from the state where they're focusing on the issue, to the place where they're aligning with you. Concentrate on finding a solution; frame their problem in a solvable way.

How to Make A Problem Solvable

1. Help identify what they've lost. What necessities or feelings are missing from their life?

2. Identify the real problem. What's a person after?

3. Something is stopping them vs. what they think is stopping them. Identify what's stopping a person; this is the problem we're making solvable.

The most effective solution to make a problem solvable is to change HOW people look at a problem.

Recognize Habitual Patterns Are

Powerful

We need to begin by tracing how a person got where they are. We do this by discovering their thoughts, feelings, actions, and emotions. Over some time, it's these continued thoughts, feelings, activities, and emotions that lead to the creation of their situation. Your ability to identify their underlying patterns will be your source for helping them with their challenge. When you see something that they can't, you're able to anticipate.

Identifying Habitual Patterns

We're all after the same six necessities. So, do you remember what makes each of us unique? It's how we fulfill our needs. How we meet what we need is dependent on how we use our map to guide us to them.

When you experience an intense emotional event, your brain wants to know where it originated. If the event gave us joy, the mind seeks more of it. If the event causes pain, the brain wants to stay away from it.

Remember: We're more motivated to protect ourselves from a painful experience than we are to have a pleasurable experience. Pain = hurt, enough hurt means damage and enough damage = death. Our brain is an ancient mechanism, whose primary job is survival.

Habitual patterns form in this way. We shape habits, based on how we filter the world, our unique belief structure, and our process of thinking. Daily situations mold our reactions, our actions, and the way we feel. Our habitual patterns can also be outdated. What served you at one time, may not be necessary anymore, and it may be causing you damage without you knowing. Habitual patterns can be useful for us, bad for us, or neutral. What are some examples of Habitual Patterns?

1. **Good Habitual Pattern:** Waking up early in the morning.

2. **Wrong Habitual Pattern:** Going to sleep early in the morning.

3. **Neutral:** The clothing we wear. You may have a pattern of dressing a certain way.

Creating & Destroying Habitual Patterns

After you've identified the habitual patterns a person is using, you can use that same pattern to create change within them. Let's say you notice a habit that's creating incredible success and fortune in someone's life. If it creates that much positivity and success in their business life, couldn't they use it to create those same results in their marriage? They sure can! Contrast that with a person who's destroying their quality of life. You can guide a person in destroying that habit and replacing it with a pattern that elevates them to new levels.

The more that you're able to consciously identify these habitual patterns, in yourself and other people, the more significant the impact you'll have in leading people to shape new models.

Here's how: Model the habitual patterns that other successful people use, what's created success for you, and what you envision will generate success in the future.

1. Identify a successful habitual pattern (*Ex: Saving to Invest*).

2. Decide to model that successful habitual pattern (*Ex:Plant your flag & decide you're going to invest like a billionaire*).

3. Create the habit in your own life (*Ex: Study one or two successful mentors who have what you want & invest the way they do*).

Effective leaders impact people on different levels. Before they can influence other people, they have to change & master themselves.

Mastering Self

- **(Level 1) Transforming your emotional frame in any situation:** Have you encountered a difficult challenge that brings out your worst self? Level 1 is the ability to take that situation and bring out your best self.

- **(Level 2) Transforming your emotional frame in a moment:** Being able to make yourself go from negative emotions to positive, instantly. You're leading yourself from moment to moment.

- **(Level 3) Transforming your emotional frame permanently:** This is where you spend most of your time at level 10+. You don't have to consciously change yourself in a moment or a situation, because you've already permanently impacted yourself. You live your best life, consciously & unconsciously. Level 3 is mastery of yourself. Once you master this, you can achieve all three of these with other people. That's where you'll reach a level of Leadership at the master level.

Causes & Effects

Life is full of causes and effects that build over time. The results of our decisions take time; we have to move in a direction for a while before we see the impact.

For example, we don't go to the gym one time (cause) and get fit for life. We have to keep going, and our body begins to transform as a result (effect). On the other hand, we don't eat one unhealthy meal (cause) and have a heart attack. We have to eat unhealthy for an extended period, which causes health problems (effect).

Remember this formula: Thoughts = feelings = actions = results.

You'll find this basic formula in The Secrets of the Millionaire Mind by T. Harv Eker (Highly

Recommend).

When you think a thought, you feel it, that feeling will determine the action you take, and your activities will determine your results. So, a *cause* is an *action*, and when you make enough **causes or actions** over time, you get a result.

The Delayed Effect

There's a period of waiting before you create an effect. You won't invest one time and wake up the next day, a multi-millionaire. It takes an accumulation of actions to create that effect. This waiting period is the delayed effect.

If you and I are anything alike, I've questioned what I'm doing many times. Like most people, I secretly wish the rewards came instantly. When you head in a direction long enough, you start to wonder if it's working for you. You may second guess your decision or move onto something else. People who do this are the ones who start a job, get super excited, and leave that same job for another one six months later. Then they get all excited and begin the cycle over again.

Another example is investing in the stock market. Some people will check their stock positions every day. They're confident when it's going up and get nervous when they see a small day to day swing in the stock. Emotions cause people to buy high and sell low, never realizing the actual value of the stock because they didn't accumulate enough actions and let the delayed effect work. Can you relate?

If you're in this place now, anxiously waiting for something to happen and not seeing the results yet, remind yourself there's a delayed effect. If you stop, you have a 100% chance of never getting where you want to go. You may be right around the corner from a breakthrough if you stay with it and let the delayed effect work.

Change The Future

How quickly can we change? Some people will

say, *"It took me five years to leave my bad relationship."* However, it took less than a second to leave the relationship, and five years to get to that point. Because we make our decisions instantly, It wasn't a 5-year process. It's our decisions that change our future, and our brains use three questions to process any situation.

How we Handle Situations

1. We determine what makes a situation unique and distinct

2. We reflect on what occurred right before this situation

3. We identify what has been consistent

     We can misinterpret these questions and create associations that aren't true.

     Example: As a child, I was timid when friends would come over. I felt embarrassed because my home wasn't as big or as lovely as my friend's homes. So, one time my friend and his older brother came to my house because they wanted to go swimming. I hid in my mom's closet because I was so shy and embarrassed about our home. Over 15 years later, when I lived on my own, I felt those same feelings of embarrassment having people over when I felt like my house wasn't the biggest or the best. I built a false association in my childhood that I had to live at a certain level for people to accept me.

It's also possible to connect pain with a situation that's good for us. When this happens, our brain mixed up its association.

Example: The Gym. Do some people link pain with the thought of going to the gym? And is it good for us? We know the answer. So why do we use strong language against the gym like: "Sweaty Gym Rats"? When we associate this strong language with something good for us, we create this mixed association in our brains and decide that the gym = pain.

Our decisions shape our future, and our choices come from the unique way we evaluate situations.

How We Make Decisions

Our brains are always deciding what the stimulus around us means. We make various associations, some true, some false, and others neutral. When we determine what a stimulus means, we make our decision. How do we decide what a stimulus means?

We ask ourselves specific questions

- **Every day we ask ourselves thousands of questions:** Whatever we ask our mind, it has to create an answer. The answer may be the truth, or the brain might make up an answer, either way, you'll get a response. It's pretty black and white; the mind doesn't come back and question whether your question makes sense. It gives you an answer.

- **What question do you ask yourself more than any other?** We each have a recurring thought; it's like the thread that guides the fabric of our lives. The most common question you ask yourself filters your life experience and focuses on what you observe or fail to see.

Your Emotional Frame

Have you ever gone to the grocery store hungry? You may have noticed you bought items you'd never usually get. It was because of your emotional frame (at that moment) changed the decisions you made.

The higher your decisions, the greater your life. Do you want to improve your experience? Improve your decision-making process.

Empowering Questions

The following list includes empowering questions for you to utilize in your daily life. The more empowering our thoughts are, the more we can strengthen and improve our lives and the lives of other people.

Answer these questions and come up with a few powerful questions for each situation. If you don't have an answer for an item, pretend you had to come up with a solution.

For example: *"If I had to feel a sense of fulfillment right now,*
what could I feel fulfilled with?"

Performance Questions

1. Did I do my best in this situation, or could I have given more effort?

2. What am I learning, or what did I learn from this experience?

3. How can I make someone's life easier?

Questions to Ask When You Wake up

1. What excites me about today? What excites me about my life?

2. What am I the most grateful for now? Who am I thankful for now?

3. Who do I love the most? What do I love the most about them?

Questions to Ask Before You go to Sleep

1. How did I make the most significant impact today?

2. Whom did I serve with my full effort?

3. What was the best learning experience I had today?

Questions That Solve Problems

1. What can I learn from this?

2. What can I enjoy/appreciate at this moment?

3. How can I make this situation closer to my ideal?

Putting This All Together

1. Getting to the root of a situation starts with identifying the habitual patterns that lead to decisions.

2. Decisions create our habitual patterns, which shape the quality of our life, how we perceive important emotional events, and the empowering or

disempowering questions we ask ourselves.

3. Once we identify the root of a problem, we can make the situation solvable. We're solving the problem when we break the continual cycle of focus. We're creating new alternatives that lead to a more exceptional quality of life, which meets necessities and creates fulfillment.

Step 5: Create Alternatives That Empower

Before a person can change, replace their old behavior. You're replacing it with a new and more empowering action that meets or exceeds their necessities. When something stops, something else must begin.

There are many ways to meet these necessities, and your job as a leader is to show people opportunities that they couldn't see and bring them options. The source of these new options is a person's experiences, imaginations, personal history, and creativity. Anyone can ask different questions and access new resources within themselves.

A powerful distinction you can use is with your words. We all have habits and patterns related to the terms we use every day. **Ex:** If I asked: how are you? You could say, "I'm good," or you could say, "I'm unbelievable." Can you see how your words would become your experience? Let's say your car broke down. You could say, "This sucks," or you could say, "This is unexpected." The words you utilize are going to affect your emotional state at that moment. What's remarkable about this is you'll make entirely different decisions depending on how you feel.

The Effects of Language

We hear ourselves speak more than anyone else. Once you hear a story enough, in your head, you may come to believe it. So what can language do for us? It can make us feel loved; it can make us feel joy, anger, and bring laughter. Words can create healing or hurt as quickly as we hear them.

In most cases, if we don't like what someone is saying, we can leave that situation. Our minds are one of the few exceptions.

Remember, the questions we ask ourselves and the words we choose to express in our thoughts and words, make up who we are.

Our minds create quicker ways to accomplish thousands of tasks. How do we know how to use an elevator? We go to our references in our thoughts and generalize how to use it. If our minds didn't create quicker ways to accomplish actions, we'd get on an elevator and have to go through our mind for a button that looked just like the elevator button. Then, we'd have to go through our brain and figure out how we pushed that exact button last time. Can you see how ineffective this is?

The generalizations we make can lift us or bring us down. Your beliefs about how to do something consist of words. When you change the terms you use, you adjust what that experience means to you.

Example: If an expression isn't in a person's vocabulary, they can't feel it. If *hate* wasn't in your vocabulary, you couldn't feel hatred, could you? No. Because you wouldn't have a reference for it.

Word Activity

Can you feel the power when you reduce negative words and enhance positive ones?

Reducing Negative words
- "I'm Depressed" vs. "I'm frazzled."

- "That sucks" vs. "That's inconvenient."

- "I was rejected" vs. "I was misunderstood."

- "I failed" vs. "I learned."

- "I hate" vs. "I prefer."

- "I'm feeling irritated" vs. "I'm feeling challenged."

Enhancing Positive Words

- "I'm determined," vs. "I'm unstoppable."

- "I feel great" vs. "I feel exceptional."

- "I enjoy" vs. "I savor."

- "That was smart" vs. "That was brilliant."

- "I'm focused" vs. "I'm incredibly sharp."

- "I'm working" vs. "I'm cranking."

How you verbalize your experience is what your experience becomes; your label becomes your reality.

When we misidentify an experience, we assign the wrong words to it. The more precise we become in identifying a narrative, the more we'll be able to change the meaning.

Example: Most people have only a limited range of words they use to describe any emotional experience. Someone might label many different experiences as "humiliating." All of those different contexts may not be humiliating; they may be inconvenient or unexpected. Whatever you call the experience becomes your experience, and you'll feel whatever you label it as. By consciously choosing how you label the situation, you can have greater control of your emotional response to it.

So, next time you feel a negative emotion, you can consciously choose how you label it. That situation will become whatever you label it as; positive or negative. You're lowering the emotional intensity, whatever the case may be.

You can also use this to enhance positive

experiences by consciously choosing more powerful words to associate with it. The same way we improved our language above.

Words create your experience. Your habitual words are forming your reality, from your thoughts, emotions, and actions.

Elevating your words will elevate your life.

Word Activity 2

What are five words that you habitually use to describe your **negative** experiences?

1.

2.

3.

4.

5.

What are five words you can replace them with to **downgrade** the experience?

1.

2.

3.

4.

5.

What's fascinating is that words describe these experiences. So, if we didn't have a term for something, we can't feel it because we can't represent it.

Word Activity 3

What are five words that you habitually use to describe your **positive** experiences?

1.

2.

3.

4.

5.

What are five words you can replace them with to **upgrade** the experience?

1.

2.

3.

4.

5.

You can enhance your positive experiences by creating an environment that supports it.

Get your friends and family on board. Ask them to watch out for you, when you're using words that don't enhance your experiences; have them bring it to your attention. Ask them if they would like to participate as well.

Example: If you say, *"I'm so angry with **X**,"* your family/friends could catch you and say, *"Are you angry, or are you a little upset?"*

These types of questions help you reflect on yourself and bring your words to your consciousness. You're empowering yourself to be able to change.

Methods To Meet Needs

What makes us unique is the methods we use to meet our necessities. Our practices can be neutral, positive, or negative. They can be methods that aren't good for us, aren't good for others, and don't serve a higher purpose (drugs, for example). Our ways can also be positive, good for us, help others, and serve a more fulfilling mission—for instance, your commitment to learn and grow.

Impactful Leadership helps people identify methods that are not meeting their necessities at a high level. When you recognize their low-level ways, you can help meet their needs with more fulfilling methods.

Let's Do This:

1. What do you love the most? Think of something that you're confident you could do for the rest of your life. Rate this on a 1-10 scale. How well does it fulfill your necessities? Please write it down.

Example: I love reading the most. It's one of my methods to meet my necessities. I could read for the rest of my life; so, this is a 10 for me. I feel extremely fulfilled because it fits all of my essentials. I'm able to give to others and serve a higher purpose by applying what I learn.

2. What's something you've put off in your life? How well is it meeting your necessities? Is it something that would be good for others and serve a higher purpose? If you had to change your mindset, so you enjoyed it, would you change the situation or change how you view the situation? Please write it down.

Example: For many years, I put off investing. It didn't feel like a way to meet my necessities. Even though it's great for others, it serves a higher purpose and allows me to do more. I changed my mindset about investing as soon as I discovered my love of growth and contribution.

How Well is Your Necessities Met?

What emotional method do you most commonly use to meet your needs?

1. How secure does your method make you feel? (Rate it 1-10) How does this method make you feel safe?

2. *How much* change and variety does this method give you? (Rate 1-10) *How does* this method make you feel a sense of change?

3. How much does your method make you feel like you matter? (Rate 1-10)

4. *How much* love do you feel from your chosen method? (Rate 1-10) *How does* your chosen method make you feel loved?

5. *How much* do you feel like you're growing with this
6. method? (Rate 1-10) *How are* you building with your way?

7. *How much* do you feel you're contributing beyond yourself?
8. (Rate 1-10) *How are* you contributing beyond

yourself?

What is Something You Can't Stand Doing?

1. Write an activity you can't stand doing:

2. Does the activity you wrote make you feel fulfilled?

On a scale of 1-10 rate, how much you get from each of these necessities:

Security:

Sense of Change:

Sense of Variety:

Love:

Growth:

Contributing beyond yourself:

Write how this activity helps or fails to improve your life and meet your necessities:

Secure:

Sense of Change:

Sense of Variety:

Love:

Growth:

Contributing beyond yourself:

Step 6: Conditioning New Behavior

When you're leading and influencing yourself or other people, we want to ensure that new behaviors and actions become lifelong habitual patterns. You can move a person at the moment, and they can revert to their old behaviors. The most potent key to conditioning a person is to help them associate their new distinctions with the emotions they desire.

Example: If you went on a memorable date and kissed in a park, every time you returned to that park, you'd associate those emotions with that decisive moment. The park is your stimulus because you've conditioned yourself to feel exceptional every time you visit it.

How do we Create These Associations?

Our associations relate to our senses. We create these associations often and were mostly unconscious in doing it. We create these associations using:

- Scent
- Visual
- Auditory
- Kinesthetics

Action Steps to Creating Associations

1. Place the person in their peak emotional frame (We'll be associating their new distinction to the way they feel).

2. In their peak emotional frame, take an unexpected action that links their distinction to the structure of emotion. **Ex: I picked my wife up when she was in a peak emotional frame. Every time I want to take her back to the height of her emotions, I pick her up.**

   Check if you associated the emotional frame

to the new behavior or action.

3. Break the cycle of emotion. We have to ensure a person can't return to their ingrained feeling.

4. Test the Association (**Ex: Picking up my wife**)

Example of how this looks: I catch my wife in a tremendous emotion or put her in it. When she's feeling at her peak emotional frame, I pick her up, which creates the association. The next time she isn't feeling at the height of her emotions, I break her cycle of feeling those bad emotions, which makes room for new feelings. Then I test the association and pick her up, which places her back in that phenomenal emotional state again.

Keys to The Associations' Success

- It must be a powerful emotional experience. In my previous example, my wife had to be feeling powerful emotions, like laughing uncontrollably.

- It must be at the climax of the emotion. In my previous example with my wife, I would take the unexpected action when she's crying laughing, not merely laughing, giving it a lasting effect.

- The unexpected action you take must be unique. It has to be a balance of different and not overly strange.

- The unexpected action you take must be duplicatable. If you can't do it again, it can't work.

Everything discussed can be applied to yourself as well.

Break an Undesired Association

(**First**) A more powerful positive association can destroy any negative association.

(**Second**) Place yourself in a peak emotional frame, and at the climax, take an unexpected action on yourself.

One of The Most Powerful Tools

One of your most excellent tools for conditioning yourself and others, for level 10+ results, is your *voice* and your *emotions*.

It's one thing to repeat in your head what you want to become. It's an entirely different world when you speak to yourself in the mirror, talking yourself into becoming the person you desire.

Speak What You Desire to Become

If you have harmful scripts on repeat in your mind, we can replace them right now with empowering scripts. Scripts that predictably return you to your very best. Sound great?

Example Scripts

- I am a champion; I am changing this world, I'm fearless, I am limitless.

- I'm on a meteoric rise to the top; nothing

can stop me because I am a success.

- I adore you (Your Name), I will do today what others won't,

to have tomorrow what others don't.

- I am a leader, and all I need is within me now.

- Repeat the scripts you choose must over and over out loud, consistently. You're commanding your mind and emotions to become what you want. Your brain and body have no choice but to obey you.

Remember: Speak what you desire to become and reinforce it with repetition.

You're developing a lifelong skill, begin right now.

Step 7: Cultivate a New Environment & Tie it to Their Greatest Purpose

Now that you've conditioned the behavior into a repeated pattern, a person can still revert to old habits, based on their environment. To solidify this new association, we need to cultivate their environment and relate it to their highest purpose in life. It has to be so strong that even the most challenging environments won't break it. We must consider a person's peers (family, friends, co-workers).

The Peer Environment

The standards of a person are often a direct reflection of their peer group. The persons' standards have a tremendous impact on their actions and behaviors. For change to last, the person's environment has to support it, including surrounding a person with a group that has high expectations and standards. Surrounded by people who elevate themselves, we upgrade ourselves.

- If four people in your group are <u>drug addicts</u>, you're likely to be 5th.

- If four people in your group are <u>millionaires</u>, you're likely to be 5th.

How do we Cultivate a New Environment?

- Join an organization that interests you.

- Get a mentor or a coach (you're doing that right now with me).

- Setup the environment to support the change (Ex: If you want to watch less T.V., get rid of the T.V.).

- Get a friend or peer to hold you accountable for your results (Ex: I like stickk.com for this).

- Consciously decide whom you're going to surround yourself with and remove toxic people.

Who Are We?

Each of us has developed a unique identity, which is how we define ourselves. We go to incredible lengths to ensure that we stay consistent with how we see ourselves. Our role as leaders is to shape the identities of the people around us, help them to grow their identity, and help them expand. Many people's character is far less than their actual potential.

Your unique identity is your belief system about who you are as a person.

How to Grow and Expand our Identities?

- **Utilize the environment to transform the identity:** When you strive to help someone grow, you must be at the level that you're challenging a person to reach. We don't judge. We lead by example. Be the environment.

- **Experiences:** Give a person an experience that makes their current identity false. For example, if a person thinks they're worthless, put them in a situation where they provide worth and value.

- **Change their body:** A person will experience the world completely different if they stand tall, with their shoulders back, take long strides, and breathe deeper. These are all within our control.

- **Changing the Emotional Frame:** We can connect a person's identity to a more empowering emotional frame.

- **For example**, I've attached my character to my drive. I live in a driven state of being, it makes me feel incredible, so I want to identify myself this way.

- **Speak what you wish to become:** You can change your identity by associating it with whatever you speak repeatedly. Remember the previous chapter? You're using your body, your mind's focus, and your words all at once.

- **Celebrate the wins:** When you do something well, or you see someone else do something well, acknowledge it. You'll associate that positive feeling with the identity. You'll become a person who notices the positive more often.

- **Target Pain Points:** Show a person how their current behaviors, thoughts, beliefs, or actions are causing tremendous pain. Then, show them how they can have immense pleasure when they make a new decision. They _must_ see the benefits. You're showing them a more exciting future with new possibilities.

- **Pretend:** Pretend as if they were a different person. Take them to the future or the past. Have them remember a time in their history when they felt invincible. How would it feel in the future? How would it look in the future? Take their mind to that place.

- **Self-Development:** Help them grow. Help people master something new and take on a new challenge. With the growth of our skills comes the expansion of whom we believe we are.

All of these distinctions are for the benefit of yourself or other people. Your influence will come from the high standards you set for yourself. When other people see that *you live* what *you say*, you'll be able to build them up by your example.

People have to feel that you love them, you're not judging and that you're challenging them to raise their standards. If you have the highest expectations in your environment, and you're the most caring; you'll be the leader.

How To Become The Leader

1. **Discipline your emotional frame:** When you set a high standard for yourself, you also have to temper your emotions in alignment with your standards.

   For example, Most people can be a leader, in times when it's easy; when there are no challenges. Although, I've seen many leaders who unravel in a stressful situation.

2. **Discovering the magnificent:** There's positivity everywhere around us. Every situation, and every context, is neutral. We assign different meanings to them, making them positive or negative. At any time, we can decide to see what's right in something, instead of what's wrong. In my sales course, *"Professional Persuasion,"* I share how to deliver sincere compliments. Discovering the magnificent is about finding the best in others and making them feel like they matter.

   Most Important: When you feel loved -like

you're doing things that matter- you can make others feel loved and significant. Leadership is sacrifice and service. It's caring for others and looking outside of ourselves. It's setting a high standard for yourself and the people around you.

Expanding Your Leadership Impact and Depth

Impact & Depth

Our goal isn't to manage; we're not managers. Our goal is to serve.

What Distinguishes Leaders from Managers?

Managers don't:

- Move the fabric of a human being, enhancing their distinctions, thoughts, feelings, actions, and beliefs. Managers can't inspire a person to act when they're not physically there, or years after they're gone. Leaders can.

- Managers can't uncover new resources within a person; managers can't shift a person **from** an emotional frame where they're down **to** a framework where they're empowered, excited, and confident in their future.

How does a Leader Accomplish This?

- Leaders identify patterns that are stopping people from their peak performance.

- Leaders take a problem that seems impossible and redefine it to make it possible.

- Leaders condition positive behavior.

- Leaders have clarity and vision. They know where they are and the end goal.

- Leaders create rapport in an environment of mutual respect and trust.

- Leaders do whatever it takes and use a person's reasons to help them achieve a breakthrough.

- Leaders introduce new possibilities (Ideas,

Tools, Strategies, Distinctions).

- Leaders understand a person's world and use tools with respect & appreciation.

Gauging Your Leadership

We're going to explore the two facets of Leadership, so you'll be able to expand and deepen your impact as a leader.

1. We'll identify your *depth* as a leader.

2. We'll identify the *impact (width)* you have as a leader.

Your Depth as a Leader (Most Important)

Your depth as a leader comes back to how you use your body, the words you use consistently, and your focus. When you master these, you're able to guide others to mastery.

First Level: Can you shift these moment to moment? The first level is the ability to make a change in actions, behavior, and emotions instantly (Shifting from Angry to centered immediately).

Second Level: Can you change your body, words, and focus on adapting to and permanently overcoming a challenging situation? This level happens over some time (you move from hating your job to transforming that same experience into pleasure).

Third Level: Can you permanently expand and evolve who you are as a whole person? Necessities, emotional habits, and guiding map. You identify your top two needs and your habitual emotions. You consciously decide your beliefs and remove disempowering beliefs.

Fourth Level: Can you replicate this, so another person masters these levels? (This is where you begin exerting influence on more than yourself, you're influencing externally).

Your Impact as a Leader (Width)

The width determines your impact as a leader by the scale (reach) to which you have mastered. How many people can you impact at once?

Level 1: You've mastered the ability to exert influence on
yourself (I get myself up early to go to the gym).

Level 2: You've mastered the ability to influence yourself and another person (I get myself and my wife up early to go to the gym).

Level 3: You've mastered the ability to influence groups of
people in that context (I lead a group of people in the gym).

Level 4: You've mastered the ability to influence and inspire people without your presence (A group of people goes to the gym consistently, as a result of my influence, without me being there).

- What is your level of impact as a leader?

- What action can you take today to expand your impact?

Where Are You Overall?

- What is your level of depth as a leader?

- What is your width of impact as a leader?

- Where are you consistently with depth and width?

Recap: Depth & Width

Depth:

First Level: Can you shift these moment to moment? The first level is the ability to make a change in actions, behavior, and emotions instantly (turning from Angry to centered immediately).

Second Level: Can you change your body, words, and focus on adapting to and permanently overcoming a challenging situation? This level happens over some time (you move from hating your job to transforming that same experience into pleasure).

Third Level: Can you permanently expand and evolve who you are as a whole person? Necessities, emotional habits, and guiding map. You identify your top two needs and your habitual emotions. You consciously decide your beliefs and remove disempowering beliefs.

Fourth Level: Can you replicate this, so another person masters these levels? (This is where you begin exerting influence on more than yourself, you're influencing externally).

Width:

First Level: You've mastered the ability to exert influence on
yourself (I get myself up early to go to the gym).

Second Level: You've mastered the ability to influence yourself and another person. (I get myself and my wife up early to go to the gym)

Third Level: You've mastered the ability to influence groups
of people in that context (I lead a group of people in the gym).

Fourth Level: You've mastered the ability to influence and inspire people without your presence. A group of people goes to the gym consistently, because of my influence, without me being there.

Your ability to go deep is more important than how many people you can reach.

Leadership means going deep and impacting people over time, with or without being there. These distinctions mark an influential leader.

A Level of Personal Honesty

At any level of personal honesty, you know better than anyone else where you're at as a leader. The starting line isn't essential because these are lifelong skills that require a commitment to long- term development. Becoming conscious of these leadership levels means you can decide the level of Leadership you want for your own life. You have the target, and you have the tools! Go for depth before you go for width, and live to serve others. All of this material I share with you has changed my personal life, and I've changed people's lives by utilizing it. This material is my "level 4" for depth and width. I live the example, and I'm confident you will as well. I'm touched that you've made it to this point.

You have everything you need to impact on a massive scale, and my promise to you is that I'll be somewhere in the world living and breathing this as well. I'm always in your corner, and I want you to reach out to me and share your successes and challenges. We're more potent as a community, and It's my honor to learn and grow with you. I've also included a BONUS chapter from my new book *You Are Rich,* which will teach you how to get anything you want from life. If you enjoyed this book or received value from it in any way, I'd like to ask you a favor. Would you honor me by leaving a review? It would be much appreciated!

With appreciation, Wes

BONUS: *YOU ARE RICH*

CHAPTER ONE: MIND CONTROL

"You can only control two things in your life: Your attitude and your actions." Darren Hardy

The ability to feel comes from our mind. The mind's often referred to as the seat of consciousness and thought, the very place of our cognitive awareness and imagination. The power and importance of the brain are absolute. Your mind controls your physical expressions, manifestations, and actions. Logical deduction says that the ability to control our mind will cause a radical change in the wellness and effectiveness of anyone.

Here's a classic example of the mind's potent influence on our success and well-being. Have you ever heard of the PLACEBO effect? A placebo effect is a fake treatment believed to be real. Doctors track patients for changes in behavior such as elevated moods and more energy. The doctor assures the patient that they'll improve. The patients' mind subconsciously believes a lie, which becomes their reality. When patients start to feel better, they get pumped up and excited about this improvement. The improvement tricks them into believing the fake drug works. Their strengthened belief, more often than not, increases the effect of the treatment until they feel cured.

Your *intention* is a robust tool that can take on a life of its own to effect radical change. Understanding that the subconscious mind controls the expression of the physical is crucial to determining your success. Thinking with *intention* is not just hypothetical. It is more than just a seat of consciousness; it is the power that drives action, will, and grit.

The subconscious mind is the sum of what we see, hear, say, and believe. Think of it like food. Some people feed their minds with "candy," others fill themselves with "apples." These people aren't totally to blame, because it comes from their childhood. Imagine a child that grew up in a family who eats two meals a day. It's typical for that child to be subconsciously satisfied with two meals a day. They *see* it as being normal; why would they change? What we see and experience shackles or elevates us.

While we're the expression of what we see, you should know that the mind's also influenced by what you say and hear. Ultimately, we're the ones that control our mind; we control what enters the brain and how it functions. We are the god of our thought process, our consciousness, and our imagination, the controllers of our minds.

Chapter Summary/Key Takeaways

In the next chapter, you'll learn and understand the underlying thought process we all go through. Now that you know that we control our thought and what goes into our minds, you will learn how to direct and channel your thinking into getting results.

Next Steps

Also by Wes Lee

You Have A Purpose

You Are Rich

You Are Free

You Are Successful

Professional Persuasion

The Brave Bunch (Children's Book)

Read more at amazon.com/author/wes_lee

About the Author

Wes Lee is a passionate advocate for success with over a decade of experience and a business degree from Hawaii Pacific University. Best known for his Leadership in the Army and operating multiple successful businesses, including lending money in 42 states, starting a business that significantly reduces health-care costs, and taking ownership in a life insurance company. Lee's books take his hard-won experience and translate it into easy recipes you can follow to achieve massive breakthroughs. His site https://twitter.com/wes_lee_success shares strategies and resources to have everything you want from life while getting paid handsomely. Wes loves living in Kapolei, Hawaii (a personal dream) with his wife and digging his toes in the sand at the lagoons of Ko'olina.

Follow at https://www.tiktok.com/@weslee1988

www.ingramcontent.com/pod-product-compliance
Lightning Source LLC
Chambersburg PA
CBHW021418210526

45463CB00001B/424